STORIES FROM ANCIENT CIVILIZATIONS

African Myths

CHERRYTREE BOOKS

Distributed in the United States by
Cherrytree Books
1980 Lookout Drive
North Mankato, MN 56001

Library of Congress Cataloguing-in-Publication Data

Shahrukh Husain.
African myths / by Shahrukh Husain and Bee Willey.
p. cm.--(Stories from ancient civilizations)
Includes index.
ISBN 978-1-84234-437-8 (alk. paper)
1. Mythology, African. 2. Tales--Africa. I. Wiley, Bee. II Title.

BL2400.S36 2007
398.2096--dc22

2006032226

First Edition
9 8 7 6 5 4 3 2 1

First published in 2006 by Evans Brothers Ltd
2A Portman Mansions, Chiltern Street, London,
W1U 6NR, United Kingdom

CREDITS
Editor: Julia Bird
Design: Robert Walster
Artworks: Bee Willey
Production: Jenny Mulvanny

African Myths

Shahrukh Husain
and Bee Willey

Introduction

Myths are probably the earliest stories ever told. People in ancient times used them to explain everything that was important in life—such as how the universe was created and how the stars, sun, moon, and planets hung in the sky. To ancient peoples, these elements were gods, whom they worshiped and whom they believed controlled their lives. It was thought that if the gods were kept happy, they would be kind to the people.

Myths tend to have a moral and are usually about important matters such as birth, death, and the afterlife. In the first story we learn how Yorubaland, believed by the Yoruba tribe to be the center of the world, was created by Oduduwa, son of the supreme god Olodumare. In another, we learn how Man and Woman came to live on Earth and upset all the animals, as well as the creator god Mulunge, with their lack of respect for their natural environment (pages 12-13). The story of Kitamba's wife (pages 28-29) illustrates the ancient African belief in the underworld, while the Spider and the Ghosts (pages 14-15) describes the ghosts that some Africans still believe lurk in the wilderness.

People in ancient times traveled huge distances, looking for food and shelter. Some races were warlike and came to invade and conquer lands that were rich and fertile. The Epic of Dausi (pages 24-27) refers to tribes who have been forced out of their homelands to wander far and wide. All these people brought their own gods and myths with them. When they settled somewhere new, an exchange took place. They introduced their gods to the local people and in turn began to worship some of theirs. So, over the years, more myths were added and sometimes the same gods were called different names and old stories blended with new ones. The early African gods were nature gods, and so the ancient myths often feature gods and goddesses of thunder, lightning, drought, and rivers.

Africa is a large continent with many different countries with dozens of their own tribes, each with its own storytelling tradition. Elements common to most of the stories are respect for wild creatures, the dangers and gifts of the bush or wilderness, and the importance of nature. Drought, which is a serious threat to the lives of people living off the land in a hot country, is also a common feature. Spiders regularly appear in African myths—perhaps because of their mysterious ability to weave webs and create a link between heaven and Earth. Probably the most famous character of African myths is the loveable Anansi, a spider god.

The myths of Africa survive through being remembered and told within families and clans, and also because the gods and goddesses are still part of African worship. Many stories have been lost and some survive only in fragments, though, thankfully, in the last couple of centuries, people have begun to write them down. Myths about many African gods and goddesses, such as Shango and Oya, have traveled out of Africa to other parts of the world such as South America and the Caribbean, where the characters have been transformed into local saints.

Contents

How Yorubaland was Created

The Yoruba people of Nigeria, West Africa, believed that Olodumare, god of the heavens, sent his children down to create the world. They created Ife, which became the center of Yorubaland and the world. This creation myth teaches the moral that it pays to be active and make the best of what you have.

OLODUMARE, GREAT GOD OF THE HEAVENS, DECIDED IT WAS TIME HIS SONS OBATALA AND ODUDUWA DID SOMETHING USEFUL.

"Step down into the world," he commanded his sons. "Here are three gifts that will help you."

The two young men took the three bags. They peered down. For miles and miles, all they could see was swirling water. So Olodumare created a palm tree and gave his sons a gentle push. They landed safely among the large fronds of the palm.

Obatala, the older brother, fumbled around among the branches. He cut a small hole in the trunk of the tree. Immediately, frothy liquid gushed out. It was sweet and it made Obatala feel good. He drank his fill of the palm wine, then fell asleep.

His brother Oduduwa was very different. He climbed down the trunk of the palm and stood in the cool water. Then he opened the first bag from his father and started to empty out some of its contents. White sand flowed onto the surface of the waters. Oduduwa opened the second bag. A chameleon scurried out. Carefully, slowly, it placed its feet, one by one, on the sand. Oduduwa watched it with interest.

"This ground is firm," he thought. "I can walk on it."

Oduduwa emptied out the remains of the second bag—it was black soil. Then he opened the third bag. Out came a chicken and began scratching around for food. Sand and soil flew in all directions, forming solid pieces of land on the water as far as the eye could see. This land came to be called Ife.

Olodumare looked down happily. His son had done well. So he sent Aje, goddess of wealth, down to Ife.

"Your father has sent you more gifts," Aje told Oduduwa. "Iron bars to make weapons, tools to prepare the Earth, and corn seeds to grow crops in it."

And that was how farming began and people could live on Earth.

When the world was created, Olodumare appointed the chief gods and they created the different Yoruba clans. The Yoruba people split into many more clans as time went on, and the gods in this story were given different names. In some myths, Oduduwa is described as a goddess who was sent down to Earth after her brother, Obatala, failed to achieve anything. Aje came along to help her.

Dzivaguru's Curse

Long ago, Dzivaguru was the mother goddess of the Shona-speaking people of Korekore in Zimbabwe. Her story answers fundamental questions about nature, such as why we have day and night, rain and drought.

DZIVAGURU LIVED IN A BEAUTIFUL PALACE BY A LAKE. Her valley was lush and filled with cattle, goats, and sheep. Her people loved her because she was kind. She brought rain to nourish the land, sunshine to warm the people, and the darkness of night for them to rest.

Nosenga, son of the sky god, looked down at Dzivaguru's wealth and her power. He was jealous.

"I will go down to Earth," he decided, "and take Dzivaguru's rich kingdom for myself."

But Dzivaguru knew what was in Nosenga's mind. She would not give up her lands without a fight. "Fog!" she commanded, "fill the valley. Light! Follow me."

Then she climbed to the top of a mountain and watched. When Nosenga arrived in her land, he was surrounded by darkness. All he could see was the shape of the distant hills and the dim glow of the sky. But that was no good. He wanted the goddess's palace and her livestock and her wonderful, glittering lake.

Nosenga knew that Dzivaguru, goddess of dark and light, owned two golden Sunbirds. To bring sunshine, she lured the birds to her and trapped the sun for while. "I won't let her beat me," Nosenga vowed. "I will trap her Sunbirds."

So Nosenga created a magical trap and soon snared both the Sunbirds. Instantly the sun began to glow in the distance and dawn broke.

Over the hills, Dzivaguru appeared. "Nosenga!" she declared. "I will punish you for snatching away my land. People will only worship you for a short time. You, too, will be replaced by outsiders. Because you trapped my Sunbirds and brought out the sun, the land will heat up and become parched. For every sin your sons commit, I will hold back the rain and drought will follow."

And with those words, Dzivaguru disappeared forever. But people remembered her words whenever there was drought or their land was invaded.

Two images of a pair of golden birds that look like swallows were found in a ruined temple in Zimbabwe about a hundred years ago. They are probably the Sunbirds mentioned in the myth of Dzivaguru. Stories in the Shona language often praise swallows for their swiftness. They migrate to Zimbabwe in spring, appearing when the sun grows stronger after winter, so they are closely connected with the sun as this myth shows.

Oya Steals Magic from Shango

Shango, the Earth god, was created at the beginning of the world when Olodumare and his sons made Yorubaland. He was immensely powerful, but he wanted even greater might. After a long time ruling the Kingdom of Oyo on Earth, he traveled up to the skies on a long golden chain.

Shango's third wife, Oya, stood before Eshu, the shaman.

"My husband has sent me to fetch the medicine you made for him," she said, offering him a goat in exchange. Eshu handed Oya a small package.

"How is it to be used?" Oya asked.

Eshu smiled. "Let Shango work it out."

Oya thanked Eshu and went on her way. But she was extremely curious.

"It won't do any harm to look," she thought, unwrapping the package.

Inside was a glowing, red powder. Oya dipped her finger into it.

"Shango won't notice if I taste a tiny bit." She popped her finger in her mouth. It was tasteless. Disappointed, Oya wrapped up the parcel and went home.

"How shall I use it?" Shango asked when Oya gave him the medicine.

Oya opened her mouth to reply, but out shot a bright tongue of fire. Eshu's magic was working!

"You stole my magic!" Shango thundered.

Terrified, Oya ran and hid among a flock of sheep. But Shango was close behind and hurled thunderstones at the sheep who had huddled around her. One by one, they fell dead and Oya hid herself among their bodies.

Shango stormed off to a nearby hill to see if there was any magic left. He opened the package. Most of the red powder was still there. He put some on his lips and took a deep breath. A tongue of fire leapt from his mouth, the same as Oya's. But he wanted to be more powerful. He took a second taste. The fire shot out further. And a third. The flames burst from his nose. Shango consumed all the magic. He breathed in, letting the air fill his lungs. Then he exhaled. Arms of fire came from his mouth and nose, catching the trees around him. They spread to the buildings until Shango's city was in flames. People ran everywhere as their homes burned down before their eyes.

Shango's people soon built a new city but people always remembered how the furious breath of Shango, Lord of Thunder, could burn down a whole city. To this day, when lightning strikes, they call "Kabiyesi!" which means "Greetings, your majesty."

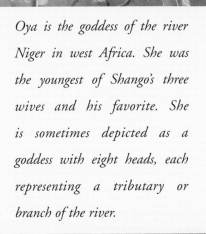

Oya is the goddess of the river Niger in west Africa. She was the youngest of Shango's three wives and his favorite. She is sometimes depicted as a goddess with eight heads, each representing a tributary or branch of the river.

Mulunge Escapes the Humans

The spider appears in many African myths, perhaps because of its ability to weave webs and spin a thread that links heaven and Earth, as in this story. This myth from Lake Malawi tells us about the beliefs of the Yao people. They hunted to survive, but showed deep respect for their natural environment and the creatures who shared it with them.

CHAMELEON WAS VERY HUNGRY. "I wonder what I"ve caught today," he thought, pulling in his trap from the river. There were two very strange creatures inside. He took the trap to Mulunge, the Creator, who had made him and all the other creatures living peacefully together in the world.

"They are humans: a Man and a Woman," Mulunge told him. "Release them from the trap and watch."

Man and Woman grew tall and strong. They took bits of wood and rubbed them together until sparks flew and they burst into flames. Man and Woman killed a buffalo, roasted it on the fire, and ate it. From that day on, they cut down trees, lit fires, and killed animals each day.

Mulunge the Creator was very upset. Man and Woman were destroying his world.

"Who will they kill next?" whispered the animals. "Who will be scorched to death on their fires?"

The creatures of the jungle became scared and took refuge all over the world. Mulunge was not afraid of the humans, but he was sad and lonely. And he no longer enjoyed living in his world.

One day, Mulunge saw Spider up in the sky.

"How did you get there, my friend?" he called out.

Spider spun him a thread and Mulunge latched on to it and climbed until he too was in the sky. And that is where he stayed because the cruelty and carelessness of humans had driven him away from the world.

The Ngombe of the Congo region tell a similar tale about their creator god escaping into the jungle from quarrelsome people. As a result, we cannot see god and do not know what he looks like. In the Barotse version from Upper Zambezi, the escaped god Nyambi becomes the sun and his wife Nasilele, the moon. In all these stories, it is the selfish behavior of humans that causes conflict and unhappiness.

The Spider and the Ghosts

Most African traditions tell us that after death, a part of us called the spirit or soul, continues to live. This may be in the most unreachable parts of a forest, beneath riverbeds, or in the darkest caves or tunnels. The souls that live longest are those of strong people such as chiefs, mothers, and much-loved people. They are happy and they stay around their families to help them.

A MAN AND HIS WIFE WERE CROSSING A RIVER WHEN THEY HEARD A VOICE. It was asking to be carried across the river. The man looked down and saw that the request had come from a skull.

"No!" said the man. "How do I know that you won't hurt me?"

"Please help it," said his wife. "It can't harm us."

When they had crossed the river, the man bent to put the skull down. But it clamped his hand in its teeth and would not let go. The skull forced the man to put it on his shoulder and walk on until they came to the bush.

"Go that way," the skull commanded.

"It looks dangerous in there," the man pleaded.

"Do as I say," hissed the skull and bit the man's neck hard. The man cried out in pain and obeyed.

Finally they came to a clearing with a few shacks falling to pieces and covered in undergrowth. Something brushed against the woman's face. She screamed and scratched at her hair. Something had become entangled in it. The next moment the air was thick with the spirits of the dead, flitting about, cheering the skull.

"Meat," they hissed. "Good food to fill our bellies."

"Fetch some wood," snarled the skull. "And don't try to run away because we can track you down by your smell, wherever you go."

"It's a fine thing you're asking us to do," snapped the man. "Why should we help you make the fire to cook us alive?"

The spirits swarmed around the couple till they could hardly breathe.

"Now, will you fetch the wood?" the skull demanded.

Quietly, the man and woman went to collect firewood. After a while, the woman sat down, weeping to herself. She grasped halfheartedly at the pile of dead twigs lying beside her. Out crawled a small spider.

"Why are you crying?" asked the spider.

"We're collecting wood," replied the woman, "so that the ghosts can light a fire to cook us on."

"I'll help you," said the spider. "But you must promise not to disturb my home again."

"Gladly," replied the man and woman together.

Immediately, the spider set to work. It spun a huge web around the clearing where the ghosts were huddled. Around and around it went, until the entire space was wrapped up in a massive web. The ghosts thrashed against it but the web held firm. They were trapped.

The man and his wife thanked the spider whole-heartedly. "You saved our lives," they said. "We promise that neither we, nor our descendants, will ever again harm a spider."

Tales from all over Africa describe ghosts as skeletons of the dead who give the illusion of having white, human bodies. They love meat, especially the flesh of humans, because they hope that it will put flesh on their own bones. They can speak to people, and, as in this story, only appear in wild, deserted places in the deep of night.

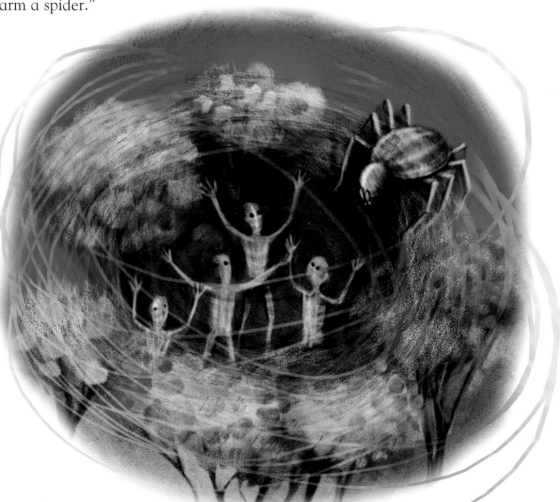

Anansi and the Stories

The Spider god Anansi is a trickster, or a culture hero—a character much loved and admired for his cleverness and his ability to get the better of others. His stories began in Ghana, West Africa, but have traveled across the world to the West Indies and parts of the Americas.

ANANSI LOVED STORIES. Everywhere he looked there were stories, terrible ones and wonderful ones, funny ones and sad ones. They made people laugh and cry and taught them to be brave and helpful and good. There was only one thing that annoyed him about stories—they belonged to someone else. So Anansi made up his mind to own all the stories in the world.

"Sell me the stories," he said to Onyame, the Supreme God, who created everything on heaven and Earth. "I will pay any price."

"Many people have asked," Onyame laughed. "But no one has brought me what I want yet."

"Then they did not want the stories as much as I do," insisted Anansi, who could never resist a challenge.

"Bring me the bees, the python, and the leopard," Onyame said. "And you will be Lord of Stories."

"I'm on my way," said Anansi, setting off. He did not stop until he came to a stream. He collected a jar of water and an empty gourd with a hole in it. He knew exactly where to find some bees and when he got there, he hurled the water at their hive. The bees scattered, buzzing loudly.

"It's raining," yelled Anansi, holding up his gourd. "Fly into this and you'll keep dry."

The bees flew into the gourd and Anansi stuffed the hole up with grass. He had captured the bees. His first task was complete.

Onyame was the supreme god of the Ashanti of West Africa. His name meant sky, but he was often worshiped in the form of a tree trunk. He was the creator god, who brought rain to the people and helped those in need. He has many other names, including Nzambi and Nyame.

Now Anansi walked deep into the jungle where the river flowed.

"Ho, Lord Python!" he called. "I need you to settle an argument."

Python crawled out from the river's edge. "Why are you shouting?" he grumbled.

"See this?" Anansi said, holding out a pole. "My wife insists you're shorter and weedier than this. I told her you are longer and sturdier."

Python shuffled forward, squinting at the pole. "I will lie beside it," he hissed. "Then you can measure me up and prove who is right."

Anansi shook his head. "My wife's a stubborn woman. She'll have to see it for herself."

So Python lay down beside the pole and Anansi bound him to it. That was the second job done.

Finally, it was time to snare the leopard. Anansi knew where Leopard hunted, so he made his way to the spot and dug a deep ditch in his path. He covered the ditch with brush, mud, and grass. Then he found a quiet hiding place and went to sleep. Very soon, he was woken by a loud roar.

"Get me out of here!"

Anansi went over to the ditch. "I would help," he called down to Leopard. "But you are vicious by nature. You'll eat me the moment you're safe."

"I won't," promised Leopard. "Help me or I'll starve to death down here."

Anansi pushed down the sturdy branch of a tree which was growing beside the ditch.

"Tie your hind legs to this," he called out, lowering a rope to Leopard. "I will hold it down."

Leopard did as Anansi asked.

"Get ready," called Anansi. Then suddenly, without warning, he let go. The branch sprung back with Leopard hanging upside down. He struggled and kicked, shouting, "Anansi, cut me down!"

"At once," replied Anansi, chuckling. He held out a sack and cut the rope. Leopard fell into it. Immediately, Anansi fastened the mouth of the sack with the rope.

Anansi's mission was complete. He took all his trophies to Onyame.

"You have proved that with determination and a little wit, you can achieve anything," Onyame said, very pleased that someone had at last brought him the creatures he had wanted for so long.

And from that day on, all stories belonged to Anansi.

Miseke and the Thunder God

This story comes from Rwanda, where the Thunder god was considered Lord of the Heavens. The elements of nature such as rain, thunder, and storms were an important part of the lives of ancient people. They made offerings to the elements in return for their favors.

KWISABA HAD GONE TO WAR AND HIS WIFE WAS TIRED AND HUNGRY. There was no one to share the household tasks while she awaited her baby's birth. A storm was coming and although she tried and tried, she could not light a fire to cook with. She looked up at the sky in despair.

"Someone, please light this fire for me," she prayed, "even if it is Thunder himself."

Lightning cracked and thunder boomed, and the next moment a tall man appeared beside her.

"I'll answer your prayer," said the man. "But in return I want your first-born if she is a daughter."

The woman agreed and the man, who was Thunder, lit her fire, chopped up a great pile of wood, and left.

Soon, the war ended. Kwisaba returned home to find his wife living in comfort with a new daughter, Miseke.

"You are indeed a daughter to be proud of," Kwisaba laughed, as he played with his baby girl. "One day, we will find you a handsome husband and get a fine bride price."

"It's time to tell him my promise to Thunder," thought Kwisaba's wife.

"We will keep Miseke safe inside the house," Kwisaba decided, when his wife had confessed. "Thunder can't take her when she's inside."

So Miseke stayed inside the house, except in fair weather when there was no sign of thunder and her parents let her play with her friends in the yard.

Miseke grew older and more beautiful and, one day, her friends noticed beads and bangles fall from her mouth as she spoke.

When a couple were to be married, it was the tradition for the groom's side of the family to pay the bride price. This was usually cattle, or some valuable grain or nuts, though in modern times it is often cash. The families met to agree the price, which was meant to be a token of respect and friendship between the two families.

"Thunder is giving Miseke gifts, just as you did when you were wooing me," her mother said to Kwisaba.

"It is time to lock her up," Kwisaba decided.

From that day on Miseke was forbidden to go out with the other girls. But one day, Kwisaba and his wife were called away on a long trip and Miseke slipped out and went to the river with her friends. Happily, they played, sang and danced until a dark cloud appeared in the sky. It rolled toward them, then dipped. There was a deep rumble, followed by lightning. The cloud scooped up Miseke in its folds, and floated swiftly up to the skies. Thunder had taken his wife. Miseke's parents were heartbroken.

"How will he treat her?" they wept. But they need not have worried. Miseke lived happily for many years with her husband and children, in a wonderful palace filled with everything she wanted. But often she thought of her parents and then she would become a little sad.

"Go to visit them," Thunder said one day, kindly. "But keep to the paths."

Overjoyed, Miseke made her way down to Earth, accompanied by her children, cattle, pots of beer, and servants to help her. Soon they arrived in the forest near her village. As they got closer, the path vanished. They were lost.

"Give me food!" a voice boomed. Before her, Miseke saw a massive oger.

"Give him the cattle!" Miseke ordered her servants.

But that was not enough. In no time at all, the oger had eaten the cattle,

drunk the beer, and swallowed the servants. Swiftly, Miseke told her eldest son to look for the river and follow its course to the village for help. She clung to the children who remained with her, praying that help would come. But by morning the oger was hungry again and began demanding Miseke's children.

Just in time came the sound of loud drum beats. Miseke saw fire brands blazing in the distance. The next moment, her father appeared out of the brush, followed by her son and other villagers.

"Miseke," they called. "You are home at last!"

Together, the men killed the oger. The village shaman cut off the oger's big toe and all Miseke's possessions suddenly reappeared before her.

Miseke's parents prepared a great wedding feast and asked Miseke and her children all about their life in the skies. But soon it was time to return. The villagers gave Miseke many presents and gathered outside to say goodbye.

Suddenly, the skies grew dark. Lightning flashed, thunder rumbled, and a great purple cloud scooped up Miseke and her children, along with all the gifts. That was the last Kwisaba and his wife saw of Miseke. But they knew she lived in comfort and bliss and that made them happy.

Monsters and ogers are found in myths from all over Africa. Most often these are giants. One particular kind of monster is portrayed as a huge mouth which shouts the word hungry, as it runs about looking for victims. People who see it are too terrified to run and the monster gobbles them up easily.

Ghasir's Lute

This story comes from the Epic of Dausi, which the anthropologist Leo Frobenius wrote between 1899 and 1915. The Epic consists of a group of songs about the mythical African city of Wagadu in West Africa, which was destroyed and rebuilt many times. The story of Ghasir and his lute is the first part. An epic is a grand tale of heroes, often told in poetry.

PRINCE GHASIR RODE BACK FROM THE BATTLE. The Borduma tribe wanted to conquer the great kingdom of Wagadu and as long as their soldiers kept attacking, Ghasir's men would fight.

"Oho Ghasir!" a voice hailed him. "Why do you go to war? You will never be king of Wagadu."

Ghasir was angry. "Show yourself!" he commanded.

An old man stepped out of the shadows.

"Kiekorri," Ghasir said, recognizing the sage. "What do you mean I'll never be king?"

"I mean what I say. You may be a brave warrior and a hero, but you will never wear your father's crown."

"You're wrong!" declared Ghasir, drawing his sword.

"Killing me will not change your fate, Ghasir," Kiekorri laughed. "It is better to go into the forest where the wild birds sing. They'll tell you what's in store for you."

Ghasir spurred his horse toward the woodland where the birds flocked. "How will I know what they say?" he wondered, as he dismounted from his horse.

As he walked toward the bushes, a large woodcock appeared in the clearing. It threw back its head and began to sing.

"I can understand its words," Ghasir realized, amazed. The bird was singing about a story. It said that it would be a mighty story, told in a song that would last forever, far beyond heroic deeds and mighty warriors because its words held the power of truth and heartbreak and love.

Ghasir was enchanted by the song. "Kiekorri," he reported back to the sage. "I heard the woodcock and understood his words."

"So that is your fate!" said Kieokorri. "Your destiny is to be a poet, not a fighter. What are you waiting for? Don't all good poets have lutes?"

Ghasir sought out the best lutemaker in all of Wagadu and when his lute was ready, he tried its strings. But the lute was silent.

"What's this?" he thundered at the lutemaker.

"I am just a craftsman," the lutemaker replied, shaking with fear because he knew that those who displeased Ghasir were likely to have their hearts impaled on a sharp weapon. "I can only craft the instrument. And this is the best I've ever made. But only creatures that bleed and breathe have a voice. Your lute will sing if you take it to battle with you. Attach it to your shoulder, let it become part of you.

The Epic tells us that Ghasir belonged to the Fasa dynasty. This may be one of the reasons that African scholar Dr. Jan Knappert writes that the mythical city of Wagadu may be the present capital of Burkina Faso, also spelled Ougadougou. In the full version of the story, the wanderings of Ghasir and his family through northern Libya, south to Niger, Benin, and Burkina Faso, may show the migration of tribes long ago.

Let your blood run through it and let it breathe your breath. Only then will it sing the song you want to hear."

Ghasir summoned his sons. "There is nothing greater than reputation," he said. "You and I, we fight every day. Our deeds end with the battle. But words live beyond us. If we want our deeds remembered, we must fight even harder to be part of a great song that will live forever."

For seven days Ghasir fought harder than ever before. So did his sons, urged on by the desire for fame. Each night Ghasir arrived home, full of sorrow, with a dead son over his shoulder. And his tears of grief mingled with the blood of his dead sons and drenched the silent lute. But the Borduma kept coming.

On the eighth day of battle, the people of Wagadu came to Ghasir. "Please end this bloody war," they pleaded. "We long for peace. You have already sacrificed seven sons for the sake of fame. Take what is left of your family and leave us in peace."

Ghasir accepted the wishes of his people and went into the bush. There, near the desert, he spent many years herding cattle.

One night, when his companions were asleep, he sat beneath the dark Sahara sky, watching the huge patterns formed by the stars. He thought of his dead sons and his father who had passed away, leaving Wagadu without a ruler. He remembered stories of how the Borduma came after he had left and his people opened the gates of Wagadu, saying they wanted peace. Yet the Borduma ravaged the crops, pillaged the granaries, and razed the houses to the ground, leaving behind only rubble and dust. Ghasir's heart filled with sadness. And then he heard a song. It was speaking his thoughts. Who was singing it?

Ghasir held out his precious lute and listened to the verses pouring from it. And tears streamed from the eyes of the warrior that had been held in since he was a child.

"It is true, after all," he wept. "This is the song that will last forever."

And so it is that the Epic of Dausi is told to this day.

Kitamba's Wife

This story from the Mbundu people of Angola shows their belief that the dead cross over to continue life in another world, often in the same form. Their god of death, Kalunga-Ngombe, lives underground, unlike other gods. Kalunga says in another story that he kills for a reason and that he is not cruel. But once someone has seen him death usually follows.

Queen Mulongo had died and her husband, King Kitamba, was so unhappy that he made the whole village mourn with him. Ordinary life had come to a standstill. So the people sent a village elder to get the advice of the kimbanda, a wise man with powerful medicine.

"The queen is dead, but we must carry on with our lives," said the elder. "What shall we do?"

The kimbanda thought a moment, then replied,

"I will go and find the queen in the kingdom of Kalunga to get her advice."

When the elder had left, the kimbanda dug a deep hole in the ground of his hut, directly in front of his fireplace. "I'm going down this hole," he told his wife. "Water it well each day I'm away so that the soils stays soft and loose. Do not stop thinking of me and keep praying for my return."

The kimbanda descended into the hole and found himself on a long road, which he followed until he came to a small group of people. Among them was Queen Mulongo, peacefully weaving a basket. The kimbanda greeted the queen politely.

"Your husband mourns you day and night," he said. "Can you return to the world of the living to comfort him?"

Mulongo looked up from her weaving. "Do you see that man on the big chair?" she asked, pointing. "He is Kalunga-Ngombe, the Lord of Death. Once he takes someone away, they can never return to the world of the living. But I am happy here."

Mulongo leaned forward and whispered a message to the kimbanda. Then she took a band from her arm and gave it to him. "This will prove to Kitamba that you have spoken to me. Eat nothing while you are in Kalunga's kingdom or you will have to remain here."

The kimbanda thanked the queen politely and returned to his home through the hole in the ground. He thanked his wife and set off immediately to see Kitamba.

"Queen Mulongo has sent you a message," he said, showing him the armband for proof. "Stop your mourning because you will meet her very soon."

Kitamba was happy again. "Let my people resume their lives," he proclaimed. "Let them pound their grain and fetch water from the river. Let their children sing and play. Mulongo and I will soon be together again."

The kimbanda in this story is a kind of shaman—a holy man, who is in touch with the spirits and has the power of healing. In times of need, his people seek his help and he is able to travel to other worlds in order to ask for the help of the gods or the dead. Sometimes this involves a burial ceremony like the one described in this story.

Glossary

Anansi – a popular trickster god who was famous for his love of getting the better of others. He is shown as being either a spider, or a human, or a combination of the two. Tales of Anansi are believed to come from the Ashanti tribe of West Africa.

Borduma – an ancient West African tribe who attacked and destroyed the mythical city of Wagadu.

Bride price – also known as a dowry, this is a sum of money that is paid by the husband or his family to the family of his future wife before they are married, as a contribution to setting up a new home. This ancient practice is still followed in some parts of the world today.

Chameleon – a lizard that is famous for being able to change the color of its skin.

Clan – a collection of tribes who are ruled by the same chief.

Culture hero – a mythical character who is much loved by people for his cleverness, trickery, and invention.

Drought – a long period of time when there is little or no rain.

Dzivaguru – the Earth goddess of the Shona-speaking people of Korekore in Zimbabwe.

Epic of Dausi – a group of songs telling the history of the mythical ancient city of Wagadu in western Africa. The story of Ghasir and his lute is the first part of the Epic.

Ghasir – the prince of Wagadu

Gourd – the hollowed-out shell of a fruit, which can be used as a cup or bottle.

Ife – according to the Yoruba people of West Africa, the center of Yorubaland where the world was created.

Kalunga-Ngombe – the god of death of the Mbundu people of Angola in southwest Africa. Unlike the other gods, he lived underground.

Kimbanda – a kind of shaman, who is believed to be able to travel to other worlds to contact the spirits.

Leo Frobenius (1873-1938) – a German explorer and archaeologist who made several journeys to Africa where he collected traditional African stories. The Epic of Dausi is one of his most famous works.

Lute – a stringed musical instrument.

Migrate – to move from one country to another. Many birds migrate in the winter in search of warmer weather.

Mulunge – the creator god of the Yao people of East Africa.

Olodumare – the Yoruba god of the heavens, who sent his sons Oduduwa and Obatala down to create the Earth.

Oya – goddess of the River Niger in West Africa and third wife of the Earth god, Shango.

Sage – a wise man.

Shango – the Earth god, created when Oduduwa and his sons made Yorubaland.

Shaman – a man who is believed to have the power to speak to the spirits, and can use this power to help his tribe.

Sunbirds – golden birds which were believed to have the power to bring sunlight.

Tribe – a group of people, often related to one another, who live together and share the same language and culture.

Yorubaland – the land created by the supreme Yoruba god Olodumare and his sons. Its center was called Ife.

Index